# CALENDAR 2023

## JANUARY
| S | M | T | W | T | F | S |
|---|---|---|---|---|---|---|
| 1 | 2 | 3 | 4 | 5 | 6 | 7 |
| 8 | 9 | 10 | 11 | 12 | 13 | 14 |
| 15 | 16 | 17 | 18 | 19 | 20 | 21 |
| 22 | 23 | 24 | 25 | 26 | 27 | 28 |
| 29 | 30 | 31 | 1 | 2 | 3 | 4 |

## FEBRUARY
| S | M | T | W | T | F | S |
|---|---|---|---|---|---|---|
| 29 | 30 | 31 | 1 | 2 | 3 | 4 |
| 5 | 6 | 7 | 8 | 9 | 10 | 11 |
| 12 | 13 | 14 | 15 | 16 | 17 | 18 |
| 19 | 20 | 21 | 22 | 23 | 24 | 25 |
| 26 | 27 | 28 | 1 | 2 | 3 | 4 |

## MARCH
| S | M | T | W | T | F | S |
|---|---|---|---|---|---|---|
| 26 | 27 | 28 | 1 | 2 | 3 | 4 |
| 5 | 6 | 7 | 8 | 9 | 10 | 11 |
| 12 | 13 | 14 | 15 | 16 | 17 | 18 |
| 19 | 20 | 21 | 22 | 23 | 24 | 25 |
| 26 | 27 | 28 | 29 | 30 | 31 | 1 |

## APRIL
| S | M | T | W | T | F | S |
|---|---|---|---|---|---|---|
| 26 | 27 | 28 | 29 | 30 | 31 | 1 |
| 2 | 3 | 4 | 5 | 6 | 7 | 8 |
| 9 | 10 | 11 | 12 | 13 | 14 | 15 |
| 16 | 17 | 18 | 19 | 20 | 21 | 22 |
| 23 | 24 | 25 | 26 | 27 | 28 | 29 |
| 30 | 1 | 2 | 3 | 4 | 5 | 6 |

## MAY
| S | M | T | W | T | F | S |
|---|---|---|---|---|---|---|
| 30 | 1 | 2 | 3 | 4 | 5 | 6 |
| 7 | 8 | 9 | 10 | 11 | 12 | 13 |
| 14 | 15 | 16 | 17 | 18 | 19 | 20 |
| 21 | 22 | 23 | 24 | 25 | 26 | 27 |
| 28 | 29 | 30 | 31 | 1 | 2 | 3 |

## JUNE
| S | M | T | W | T | F | S |
|---|---|---|---|---|---|---|
| 28 | 29 | 30 | 31 | 1 | 2 | 3 |
| 4 | 5 | 6 | 7 | 8 | 9 | 10 |
| 11 | 12 | 13 | 14 | 15 | 16 | 17 |
| 18 | 19 | 20 | 21 | 22 | 23 | 24 |
| 25 | 26 | 27 | 28 | 29 | 30 | 1 |

## JULY
| S | M | T | W | T | F | S |
|---|---|---|---|---|---|---|
| 25 | 26 | 27 | 28 | 29 | 30 | 1 |
| 2 | 3 | 4 | 5 | 6 | 7 | 8 |
| 9 | 10 | 11 | 12 | 13 | 14 | 15 |
| 16 | 17 | 18 | 19 | 20 | 21 | 22 |
| 23 | 24 | 25 | 26 | 27 | 28 | 29 |
| 30 | 31 | 1 | 2 | 3 | 4 | 5 |

## AUGUST
| S | M | T | W | T | F | S |
|---|---|---|---|---|---|---|
| 30 | 31 | 1 | 2 | 3 | 4 | 5 |
| 6 | 7 | 8 | 9 | 10 | 11 | 12 |
| 13 | 14 | 15 | 16 | 17 | 18 | 19 |
| 20 | 21 | 22 | 23 | 24 | 25 | 26 |
| 27 | 28 | 29 | 30 | 31 | 1 | 2 |

## SEPTEMBER
| S | M | T | W | T | F | S |
|---|---|---|---|---|---|---|
| 27 | 28 | 29 | 30 | 31 | 1 | 2 |
| 3 | 4 | 5 | 6 | 7 | 8 | 9 |
| 10 | 11 | 12 | 13 | 14 | 15 | 16 |
| 17 | 18 | 19 | 20 | 21 | 22 | 23 |
| 24 | 25 | 26 | 27 | 28 | 29 | 30 |

## OCTOBER
| S | M | T | W | T | F | S |
|---|---|---|---|---|---|---|
| 1 | 2 | 3 | 4 | 5 | 6 | 7 |
| 8 | 9 | 10 | 11 | 12 | 13 | 14 |
| 15 | 16 | 17 | 18 | 19 | 20 | 21 |
| 22 | 23 | 24 | 25 | 26 | 27 | 28 |
| 29 | 30 | 31 | 1 | 2 | 3 | 4 |

## NOVEMBER
| S | M | T | W | T | F | S |
|---|---|---|---|---|---|---|
| 29 | 30 | 31 | 1 | 2 | 3 | 4 |
| 5 | 6 | 7 | 8 | 9 | 10 | 11 |
| 12 | 13 | 14 | 15 | 16 | 17 | 18 |
| 19 | 20 | 21 | 22 | 23 | 24 | 25 |
| 26 | 27 | 28 | 29 | 30 | 1 | 2 |

## DECEMBER
| S | M | T | W | T | F | S |
|---|---|---|---|---|---|---|
| 26 | 27 | 28 | 29 | 30 | 1 | 2 |
| 3 | 4 | 5 | 6 | 7 | 8 | 9 |
| 10 | 11 | 12 | 13 | 14 | 15 | 16 |
| 17 | 18 | 19 | 20 | 21 | 22 | 23 |
| 24 | 25 | 26 | 27 | 28 | 29 | 30 |
| 31 | 1 | 2 | 3 | 4 | 5 | 6 |

I0389096

**Charm is deceitful and beauty is vain, but a women who fears the Lord is to be praised – Proverbs 31:30**

## JANUARY 2023

| Su | Mo | Tu | We | Th | Fr | Sa |
|----|----|----|----|----|----|----|
| 1  | 2  | 3  | 4  | 5  | 6  | 7  |
| 8  | 9  | 10 | 11 | 12 | 13 | 14 |
| 15 | 16 | 17 | 18 | 19 | 20 | 21 |
| 22 | 23 | 24 | 25 | 26 | 27 | 28 |
| 29 | 30 | 31 |    |    |    |    |

# January

## What Did She Say?

| Sunday | Monday | Tuesday | Wednesday |
|---|---|---|---|
| 1 | 2 | 3 | 4 |
| 8 | 9 | 10 | 11 |
| 15 | 16 | 17 | 18 |
| 22 | 23 | 24 "The serpent tricked me, and I ate." Genesis 3:13 | 25 |
| 29 | 30 | 31 | "We may eat of the fruit of the trees in the garden; but God said, "You shall not eat of the fruit of the tree that is in the middle of the garden, nor shall you touch it, or you shall die.'" Genesis 3:2-3 |

Dialoguing With Women in the Bible

# 2023

EVE- "God has appointed for me another child instead of Abel, because Cain killed him" Genesis 4:25

| Thursday | Friday | Saturday | Notes |
|---|---|---|---|
| 5 | 6 | 7 | |
| 12 | 13 | 14 | |
| 19 | 21 | 22 | |
| 26 | 27 | 28 | |
| What did she hear? "You will not die...your eyes will be opened, and you will be like God, knowing good and evil" Genesis 3:4-5 | | "I have produced a man with the help of the Lord" Genesis 4:1 | |

Dialoguing With Women in the Bible

# WHAT DID THEY SAY? HOW WOULD YOU RESPOND?

Take a look at the following passages. Investigate each woman's life situation that led to her statement. Comment on her statement and how it made you feel. Considering the same scenario, what would you say?

Potiphar's Wife = Genesis 39 - " Lie with me!"

Rebekah = Genesis 24 ; Genesis 25:22; Genesis 27 - "Let your curse be on me"

**Consider it pure joy, my brothers and sisters, whenever you face trials of many kinds, the testing of your faith produces perseverance – James 1:2–4**

## FEBRUARY 2023

| Su | Mo | Tu | We | Th | Fr | Sa |
|----|----|----|----|----|----|----|
|    |    |    | 1  | 2  | 3  | 4  |
| 5  | 6  | 7  | 8  | 9  | 10 | 11 |
| 12 | 13 | 14 | 15 | 16 | 17 | 18 |
| 19 | 20 | 21 | 22 | 23 | 24 | 25 |
| 26 | 27 | 28 |    |    |    |    |

# February — What Did They Say?

| Sunday | Monday | Tuesday | Wednesday |
|---|---|---|---|
| "Our father died in the wilderness; he was not among the company of those who gathered themselves together against the Lord | in the company of Korah, but died for his own sin; and he had no sons." Numbers 27: 1-3 | | 1 |
| 5 | 6 | 7 | 8 |
| 12 | 13 | 14 | 15 |
| 19 | 20 | 21 | 22 |
| 26 | 27 | 28 | |
| Mahlah | Noah | Hoglah | Milcah |

Dialoguing With Women in the Bible

# 2023

"Why should the name of our father be taken away from his clan because he had no son? Give to us a possession among our father's brother ." Numbers 27: 3-4

| Thursday | Friday | Saturday | Notes |
|---|---|---|---|
| 2 | 3 | 4 | |
| 9 | 10 | 11 | |
| 16 | 17 | 18 | |
| 23 | 24 | 25 | |
| | The first women recorded in the Bible to challenge the inheritance laws for women among men in the same situation. | What did they hear? Moses listened, he petitioned God for the right thing to do, and then he granted them the some property- Numbers 27: 5-11 | |

Tizah

Dialoguing With Women in the Bible

# WHAT DID THEY SAY? HOW WOULD YOU RESPOND?

Take a look at the following passages. Investigate each woman's life situation that led to her statement. Comment on her statement and how it made you feel. Considering the same scenario, what would you say?

Herodias's Daughter (Salome) = Matthew 14:1-12; Mark 6:17-28

_____
_____
_____
_____
_____
_____
_____

The Bleeding Woman = Matthew 9:20-22; Mark 5:25-34; Luke 8:43-48

_____
_____
_____
_____
_____
_____
_____
_____
_____

**Focus on enjoying the present. There is no point in dwelling on 'what if....?' – Matthew 6:34**

## MARCH 2023

| Su | Mo | Tu | We | Th | Fr | Sa |
|----|----|----|----|----|----|----|
|    |    |    | 1  | 2  | 3  | 4  |
| 5  | 6  | 7  | 8  | 9  | 10 | 11 |
| 12 | 13 | 14 | 15 | 16 | 17 | 18 |
| 19 | 20 | 21 | 22 | 23 | 24 | 25 |
| 26 | 27 | 28 | 29 | 30 | 31 |    |

# March

## What did she say?

| Sunday | Monday | Tuesday | Wednesday |
|---|---|---|---|
| "I am running away from my mistress Sarai" Genesis 16:7-8 | Hagar | | 1 |
| 5 | 6 | 7 | 8 |
| 12 | 13 | 14 | 15 |
| 19 | 20 | 21 | 22 |
| 26 | 27 | 28 | 29 |

Dialoguing With Women in the Bible

# 2023

**"Do not let me look on the death of my child"**
Genesis 21:16

| Thursday | Friday | Saturday | Notes |
|---|---|---|---|
| 2 | 3 | 4 | |
| 9 | 10 | 11 | |
| 16 | 17 | 18 | |
| 23 | 24 | 25 | |
| 30 | 31 | "You are El-roi !"  "Have I really seen God and remained alive after seeing him?" Genesis 16:13 | |

Dialoguing With Women in the Bible

# WHAT DID THEY SAY? HOW WOULD YOU RESPOND?

Take a look at the following passages. Investigate each woman's life situation that led to her statement. Comment on her statement and how it made you feel. Considering the same scenario, what would you say?

The Woman caught in Adultery = John 8:1-11

_____
_____
_____
_____
_____
_____
_____

Mary of Bethany = Luke 10:38-42; John 11:1-45; John 12: 1-8

_____
_____
_____
_____
_____
_____
_____
_____

So you will find favor and good success in the sight of God and man. Trust in the Lord with all your heart, and do not lean on your own understanding. Proverbs 2:4–6

## APRIL 2023

| Su | Mo | Tu | We | Th | Fr | Sa |
|----|----|----|----|----|----|----|
|    | 1  | 2  | 3  | 4  | 5  | 6  |
| 7  | 8  | 9  | 10 | 11 | 12 | 13 |
| 14 | 15 | 16 | 17 | 18 | 19 | 20 |
| 21 | 22 | 23 | 24 | 25 | 26 | 27 |
| 28 | 29 | 30 | 31 |    |    |    |

# April

## What did they say?

| Sunday | Monday | Tuesday | Wednesday |
|---|---|---|---|
| So the king of Egypt summoned the midwives and said to them, "Why have you done this, and allowed the boys to live?" | Shiphrah | Puah | |
| 2 | 3 | 4 | 5 |
| 9 | 10 | 11 | 12 |
| 16 | 17 | 18 | 19 |
| 23 / 30 | 24 | 25 | 26 |

Dialoguing With Women in the Bible

# 2023

"Because the Hebrew women are not like the Egyptian women' for they are vigorous and give birth before the midwife come to them." Exodus 1:18-19

| Thursday | Friday | Saturday | Notes |
|---|---|---|---|
|  |  | 1 |  |
| 6 | 7 | 8 |  |
| 13 | 14 | 15 |  |
| 20 | 21 | 22 |  |
| 27 | 28 | 29 |  |

Dialoguing With Women in the Bible

# WHAT DID THEY SAY?
# HOW WOULD YOU RESPOND?

Take a look at the following passages. Investigate each woman's life situation that led to her statement. Comment on her statement and how it made you feel. Considering the same scenario, what would you say?

Samaritan Woman = John 4:1-42

_____
_____
_____
_____
_____
_____
_____
_____
_____
_____

The Fortune-teller = Acts 16:16-19

_____
_____
_____
_____
_____
_____
_____
_____
_____

**Cast your burden on the Lord, and He will sustain you; He will never permit the righteous to be moved – Psalm 55:22**

# MAY  2023

| Su | Mo | Tu | We | Th | Fr | Sa |
|----|----|----|----|----|----|----|
|    |    |    | 1  | 2  | 3  | 4  |
| 5  | 6  | 7  | 8  | 9  | 10 | 11 |
| 12 | 13 | 14 | 15 | 16 | 17 | 18 |
| 19 | 20 | 21 | 22 | 23 | 24 | 25 |
| 26 | 27 | 28 |    |    |    |    |

# May

## What did she say?

| Sunday | Monday | Tuesday | Wednesday |
|---|---|---|---|
| The Priest of Midian's Daughters | 1 | 2 | 3 |
| 7 | 8 | 9 | 10 |
| 14 | 15 | 16 | 17 |
| 21 | 22 | 23 | 24 |
| 25 | 26 | 30 | 31 |

Dialoguing With Women in the Bible

# 2023

"An Egyptian helped us against the shepherds; he even drew water for us and watered the flock." Exodus 2:19

| Thursday | Friday | Saturday | Notes |
|---|---|---|---|
| 4 | 5 | 6 | |
| 11 | 12 | 13 | |
| 18 | 19 | 20 | |
| 25 | 26 | 27 | |
| | | | |

Dialoguing With Women in the Bible

# WHAT DID THEY SAY?
# HOW WOULD YOU RESPOND?

Take a look at the following passages. Investigate each woman's life situation that led to her statement. Comment on her statement and how it made you feel. Considering the same scenario, what would you say?

The Witch of Endor = 1 Samuel 28

Abigail = 1 Samuel 25; 2 Samuel 2:2, 3:3; 1 Chronicles 3:1

**Humble yourselves under the mighty hand of God so that at the proper time he may exalt you, casting all your cares on him, because he cares for you – 1 Peter 5:6-7**

# JUNE      2023

| Su | Mo | Tu | We | Th | Fr | Sa |
|----|----|----|----|----|----|----|
|    |    |    |    | 1  | 2  | 3  |
| 4  | 5  | 6  | 7  | 8  | 9  | 10 |
| 11 | 12 | 13 | 14 | 15 | 16 | 17 |
| 18 | 19 | 20 | 21 | 22 | 23 | 24 |
| 25 | 26 | 27 | 28 | 29 | 30 |    |

# June — What did she say?

| Sunday | Monday | Tuesday | Wednesday |
|---|---|---|---|
| "Let this thing be done for me: Grant me two months, so that I may go and wander on the mountains, and bewail my virginity, my companions and I." Judges 11:37 | Jephthah's Daughter | | |
| 4 | 5 | 6 | 7 |
| 11 | 12 | 13 | 14 |
| 18 | 19 | 20 | 21 |
| 25 | 26 | 27 | 28 |

Dialoguing With Women in the Bible

# 2023

"My father, if you have opened your mouth to the LORD, do to me according to what has gone out of your mouth." Judges 11: 36

| Thursday | Friday | Saturday | Notes |
|---|---|---|---|
| 1 | 2 | 3 | |
| 8 | 9 | 10 | |
| 15 | 16 | 17 | |
| 22 | 23 | 24 | |
| 29 | 30 | | |

Dialoguing With Women in the Bible

# WHAT DID THEY SAY? HOW WOULD YOU RESPOND?

Take a look at the following passages. Investigate each woman's life situation that led to her statement. Comment on her statement and how it made you feel. Considering the same scenario, what would you say?

Mary Magdalene = Matthew 27:55-61, Matthew 28: 1-10, Mark 15: 40-47, Mark 16: 1-11; Luke 8:1-3, Luke 24:1-12; John 19:25, John 20: 1-18

**God is in the midst of her; she shall not be moved: God shall help her, and that right early – Psalm 46:5**

## JULY 2023

| Su | Mo | Tu | We | Th | Fr | Sa |
|----|----|----|----|----|----|----|
|    |    |    |    |    |    | 1  |
| 2  | 3  | 4  | 5  | 6  | 7  | 8  |
| 9  | 10 | 11 | 12 | 13 | 14 | 15 |
| 16 | 17 | 18 | 19 | 20 | 21 | 22 |
| 23 | 24 | 25 | 26 | 27 | 28 | 29 |
| 30 | 31 |    |    |    |    |    |

# July — What did she say?

| Sunday | Monday | Tuesday | Wednesday |
|---|---|---|---|
| Delilah | | | |
| 2 | 3 | 4 | 5 |
| 9 | 10 | 11 | 12 |
| 16 | 17 | 18 | 19 |
| 23 / 30 | 24 / 31 | 25 | 26 |

Dialoguing With Women in the Bible

# 2023

"Please tell me what makes your strength so great, and how you could be bound, so that one could subdue you." Judges 16:6, 10

| Thursday | Friday | Saturday | Notes |
|---|---|---|---|
| The Philistines are upon you, Samson!" Judges 16:9 | "You have mocked me and told me lies; please tell me how you could be bound." Judges 16:10; 13 | 1 | |
| 6 | 7 | 8 | |
| 13 | 14 | 15 | |
| 20 | 21 | 22 | |
| 27 | 28 | 29 | |

Dialoguing With Women in the Bible

# WHAT DID THEY SAY? HOW WOULD YOU RESPOND?

Take a look at the following passages. Investigate each woman's life situation that led to her statement. Comment on her statement and how it made you feel. Considering the same scenario, what would you say?

Bathsheba = 2 Samuel 11-12.; 1 Kings 1:15-31; 1 Kings 1-2; 1 Chronicles 3:5

_____
_____
_____
_____
_____
_____
_____
_____

Michal = 1 Samuel 18-19, 25:44; 2 Samuel 3:13-14, 6:14-23; 1 Chronicles 15:29

_____
_____
_____
_____
_____
_____
_____
_____

**But by the grace of God I am what I am: and his grace which was bestowed upon me was not in vain – 1 Corinthians 15:10**

## AUGUST 2023

| Su | Mo | Tu | We | Th | Fr | Sa |
|---|---|---|---|---|---|---|
|  |  | 1 | 2 | 3 | 4 | 5 |
| 6 | 7 | 8 | 9 | 10 | 11 | 12 |
| 13 | 14 | 15 | 16 | 17 | 18 | 19 |
| 20 | 21 | 22 | 23 | 24 | 25 | 26 |
| 27 | 28 | 29 | 30 | 31 |  |  |

# August

## What did she say?

| Sunday | Monday | Tuesday | Wednesday |
|---|---|---|---|
| The Servant girl of Naaman's Wife | | 1 | 2 |
| 6 | 7 | 8 | 9 |
| 13 | 14 | 15 | 16 |
| 20 | 21 | 22 | 23 |
| 27 | 28 | 29 | 30 |

Dialoguing With Women in the Bible

# 2023

"If only my lord were with the prophet who is in Samaria! He would cure him of his leprosy." 2 Kings 5:2-4

| Thursday | Friday | Saturday | Notes |
|---|---|---|---|
| 3 | 4 | 5 | |
| 10 | 11 | 12 | |
| 17 | 18 | 19 | |
| 24 | 25 | 26 | |
| 31 | | | |

Dialoguing With Women in the Bible

# WHAT DID THEY SAY? HOW WOULD YOU RESPOND?

Take a look at the following passages. Investigate each woman's life situation that led to her statement. Comment on her statement and how it made you feel. Considering the same scenario, what would you say?

Sapphira = Acts 5:1-11

_____
_____
_____
_____
_____
_____
_____
_____

Lydia = Acts 16:13-15

_____
_____
_____
_____
_____
_____
_____
_____

I will praise thee; for I am fearfully and wonderfully made: marvelous are yours works; and that my soul knows right well  – Psalm 139:14

# SEPTEMBER  2023

| Su | Mo | Tu | We | Th | Fr | Sa |
|----|----|----|----|----|----|----|
|    |    |    |    |    | 1  | 2  |
| 3  | 4  | 5  | 6  | 7  | 8  | 9  |
| 10 | 11 | 12 | 13 | 14 | 15 | 16 |
| 17 | 18 | 19 | 20 | 21 | 22 | 23 |
| 24 | 25 | 26 | 27 | 28 | 29 | 30 |

# September — What did she say?

| Sunday | Monday | Tuesday | Wednesday |
|---|---|---|---|
| King Belshazzar's Mother | | | |
| 3 | 4 | 5 | 6 |
| 10 | 11 | 12 | 13 |
| 17 | 18 | 19 | 20 |
| 24 | 25 | 26 | 27 |

Dialoguing With Women in the Bible

# 2023

**Now let Daniel be called, and he will give the interpretation." Daniel 5:10-12**

| Thursday | Friday | Saturday | Notes |
|---|---|---|---|
|  | 1 | 2 |  |
| 7 | 8 | 9 |  |
| 14 | 15 | 16 |  |
| 21 | 22 | 23 |  |
| 24 | 25 | 30 |  |

Dialoguing With Women in the Bible

# WHAT DID THEY SAY? HOW WOULD YOU RESPOND?

Take a look at the following passages. Investigate each woman's life situation that led to her statement. Comment on her statement and how it made you feel. Considering the same scenario, what would you say?

The Woman at the Gate = John 18:1-18

Martha of Bethany = Luke 10:38-42, John 11:1-45, John 12:1-8

**Have not I commanded thee? Be strong and of good courage; be not afraid, neither be dismayed; for the Lord your God is with you wherever you go  – Joshua 1:9**

## OCTOBER 2023

| Su | Mo | Tu | We | Th | Fr | Sa |
|----|----|----|----|----|----|----|
| 1  | 2  | 3  | 4  | 5  | 6  | 7  |
| 8  | 9  | 10 | 11 | 12 | 13 | 14 |
| 15 | 16 | 17 | 18 | 19 | 20 | 21 |
| 22 | 23 | 24 | 25 | 26 | 27 | 28 |
| 29 | 30 | 31 |    |    |    |    |

# October — What did she say?

| Sunday | Monday | Tuesday | Wednesday |
|---|---|---|---|
| Job's Wife 1 | 2 | 3 | 4 |
| 8 | 9 | 10 | 11 |
| 15 | 16 | 17 | 18 |
| 22 | 23 | 24 | 25 |
| 29 | 30 | 31 | |

Dialoguing With Women in the Bible

# 2023

"Do you still persist in your integrity? Curse God, and die."
Job 2:9

| Thursday | Friday | Saturday | Notes |
|---|---|---|---|
| 5 | 6 | 7 | |
| 12 | 13 | 14 | |
| 19 | 20 | 21 | |
| 26 | 27 | 28 | |

Dialoguing With Women in the Bible

# WHAT DID THEY SAY? HOW WOULD YOU RESPOND?

Take a look at the following passages. Investigate each woman's life situation that led to her statement. Comment on her statement and how it made you feel. Considering the same scenario, what would you say?

Elizabeth = Luke 1

Herodias = Matthew 14:1-11; Mark 6:17-28 ; Luke 3:19

**For as the woman is of the man, even so is the man also by the woman; but all things of God – 1 Corinthians 11:12**

## NOVEMBER 2023

| Su | Mo | Tu | We | Th | Fr | Sa |
|----|----|----|----|----|----|----|
|    |    |    | 1  | 2  | 3  | 4  |
| 5  | 6  | 7  | 8  | 9  | 10 | 11 |
| 12 | 13 | 14 | 15 | 16 | 17 | 18 |
| 19 | 20 | 21 | 22 | 23 | 24 | 25 |
| 26 | 27 | 28 | 29 | 30 |    |    |

# November — what did she say?

| Sunday | Monday | Tuesday | Wednesday |
|---|---|---|---|
| The Shunammite Woman | | | 1 |
| 5 | 6 | 7 | 8 |
| 12 | 13 | 14 | 15 |
| 19 | 20 | 21 | 22 |
| 26 | 27 | 28 | 29 |

Dialoguing With Women in the Bible

# 2023

"Did I ask my lord for a son? Did I not say, Do not mislead me?" 2 Kings 4:28

| Thursday | Friday | Saturday | Notes |
|---|---|---|---|
| 2 | 3 | 4 | |
| 9 | 10 | 11 | |
| 16 | 17 | 18 | |
| 23 | 24 | 25 | |
| 30 | | | |

"It is all right." 2 Kings 4:23, 26

Dialoguing With Women in the Bible

# WHAT DID THEY SAY? HOW WOULD YOU RESPOND?

Take a look at the following passages. Investigate each woman's life situation that led to her statement. Comment on her statement and how it made you feel. Considering the same scenario, what would you say?

The Women at the Tomb: Mary Magdalene; Mary, the Mother of James

Salome, the Mother of the Sons of Zebedee = Mark 16:1-8

**And blessed is she that believed: for there shall be a performance of those things which were told her form the Lord   - Luke 1:45**

## DECEMBER 2023

| Su | Mo | Tu | We | Th | Fr | Sa |
|----|----|----|----|----|----|----|
|    |    |    |    |    | 1  | 2  |
| 3  | 4  | 5  | 6  | 7  | 8  | 9  |
| 10 | 11 | 12 | 13 | 14 | 15 | 16 |
| 17 | 18 | 19 | 20 | 21 | 22 | 23 |
| 24 | 25 | 26 | 27 | 28 | 29 | 30 |
| 31 |    |    |    |    |    |    |

# December — What did they say?

| Sunday | Monday | Tuesday | Wednesday |
|---|---|---|---|
| Women of Israel | | | |
| 3 | 4 | 5 | 6 |
| 10 | 11 | 12 | 13 |
| 17 | 18 | 19 | 20 |
| 24 / 31 | 25 | 26 | 27 |

Dialoguing With Women in the Bible

# 2023

"Saul has killed his thousands, and David his ten thousands." 1 Samuel 18:6-7

| Thursday | Friday | Saturday | Notes |
|---|---|---|---|
|  | 1 | 2 | |
| 7 | 8 | 9 | |
| 14 | 15 | 16 | |
| 21 | 22 | 23 | |
| 28 | 29 | 30 | |

Dialoguing With Women in the Bible

# WHAT DID THEY SAY? HOW WOULD YOU RESPOND?

Take a look at the following passages. Investigate each woman's life situation that led to her statement. Comment on her statement and how it made you feel. Considering the same scenario, what would you say?

Mary, the Mother of Jesus = Matthew 1:16-23, Matthew 2:11,

Matthew 12:46-50, 13-54-58; Mark 3:31-35, 6:1=6; Luke 1:26-56, 2:1-52,

Mark 8:19-21; John 2:1-12, 19:25-27; Acts 1:12-14

# Phone and Email List

| Name | Cell Phone Number | E-mail Address |
|------|-------------------|----------------|
|      |                   |                |
|      |                   |                |
|      |                   |                |
|      |                   |                |
|      |                   |                |
|      |                   |                |
|      |                   |                |
|      |                   |                |
|      |                   |                |
|      |                   |                |
|      |                   |                |
|      |                   |                |
|      |                   |                |
|      |                   |                |
|      |                   |                |

# MONTHLY BUDGET
## At a Glance

MONTH OF

TOTAL INCOME                                    OTHER INCOME / SAVINGS

| EXPENSES ITEM | BUDGET | ACTUAL | DIFFERENCE | NOTES |
|---|---|---|---|---|
| MORTGAGE/RENT | | | | |
| HOUSEHOLD MAINTENANCE | | | | |
| TAXES | | | | |
| INSURANCE | | | | |
| ELECTRICITY | | | | |
| WATER | | | | |
| SEWAGE | | | | |
| GAS | | | | |
| PHONE | | | | |
| TRASH | | | | |
| CABLE | | | | |
| CELL PHONE | | | | |
| GROCERIES | | | | |
| ENTERTAINMENT | | | | |
| CHARITY/DONATIONS | | | | |
| FUEL | | | | |
| AUTO INSURANCE | | | | |
| CAR PAYMENT | | | | |
| CHILD CARE | | | | |
| CREDIT CARDS/DEBT | | | | |
| LOANS | | | | |
| DINING OUT | | | | |
| SPORTING EVENTS | | | | |
| LIVE THEATER | | | | |
| CONCERTS | | | | |
| MOVIES | | | | |
| | | | | |
| | | | | |
| | | | | |
| | | | | |
| | | | | |
| TOTAL EXPENSES | | | | |

www.ingramcontent.com/pod-product-compliance
Lightning Source LLC
Chambersburg PA
CBHW081757100526
44592CB00015B/2474